Contents

Abuja: Fresh Hopes

▲ *Cranes are a common sight in Abuja, the rapidly growing new capital of Nigeria.*

On 13 December 1991, Nigerians living in Abuja woke up to find themselves living in the new capital of their country. After years of planning and construction, Abuja had finally become the capital of Nigeria, replacing Lagos in the south of the country. But the change of the capital was about much more than building a new city. Its location in the centre of the country was important too. Nigeria is a country whose population and society are divided by differences between the north and the south. In the past, these divisions have led to many conflicts between the different religious and ethnic groups living there.

Abuja was chosen to bring an end to the troubles of the past. The city was built on land independent of any ethnic or religious group and its central location was to be a symbol of greater cooperation between all Nigerians. Despite the new start, however, Nigeria remains a divided country, not just by religion and ethnic groups, but by wealth and well-being too. Only a minority of the population enjoy the wealth and opportunity that the country offers. Millions of others are trapped in poverty, many of them struggling to survive day by day. Nigeria may have a new capital, but the politicians who occupy its plush new offices still have much to do. The economy is struggling, the environment is suffering and the population continues to grow at an alarming rate. The challenge is great, but Abuja remains a symbol of hope and change as Nigerians look forward to a better future.

▼ *The Central Mosque is built close to the Christian National Church in Abuja. Their proximity symbolizes the new era of co-operation between religions.*

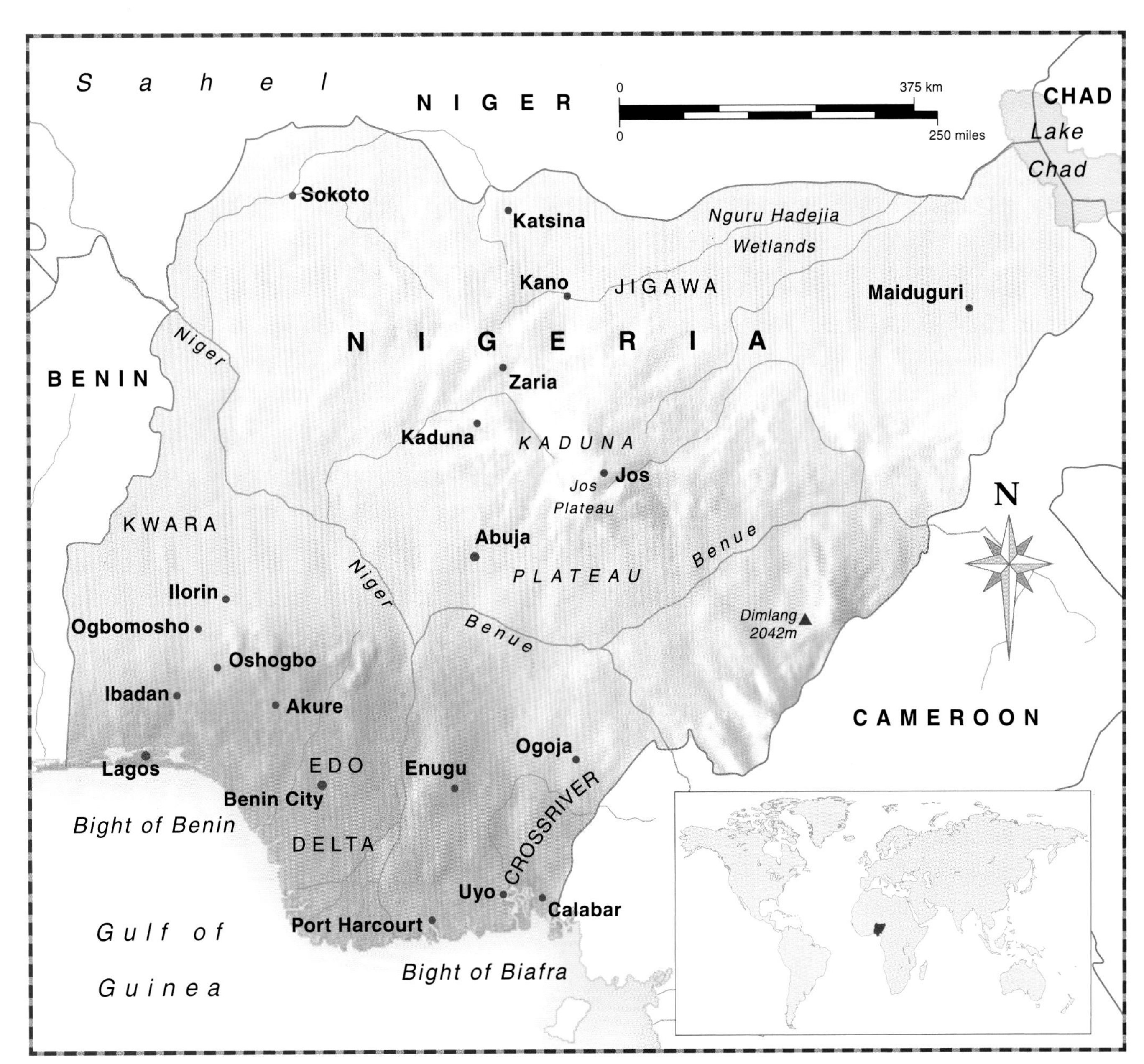

▲ *This map shows the places mentioned in this book and other major features of Nigeria.*

NIGERIA: KEY FACTS

Area: 923,768 sq km
Population: 113,862,000 (2000)
Population density: 123 people per square km
Capital: Abuja (population 0.42 million in 2001)
Other main cities: Lagos (8.7 million), Ibadan (1.6 million), Ogbomosho (0.8 million)
Highest mountain: Mount Dimlang (2,042 m)
Longest river: Niger (4,200 km)
Main languages: English, Hausa, Yoruba, Igbo and over 400 other African languages
Major religions: Muslim 50%, Christian 40%, traditional beliefs 10%
Currency: Naira (100 kobo = 1 Naira (NGN))

2 Past Times

The land that is now Nigeria has a long history of human civilization. The Nok civilization, for example, lived around the area of modern-day Jos as long as 2,500 years ago. From the eighth century several kingdoms ruled different parts of Nigeria. The most famous of these was the Benin Kingdom whose bronze and ivory sculptures were among the finest in Africa. The Benin Kingdom grew wealthy from trade in cloth, spices, and metals. From the fifteenth century, they also traded slaves with the Portuguese and later the British.

▲ *These beautiful cats are fine examples of Nigeria's famous Benin sculptures.*

In 1900 the Benin Kingdom became part of the British-controlled protectorate of Southern Nigeria. The British also controlled the protectorate of northern Nigeria and in 1914 the two were merged to form the Nigerian colony. The British ruled Nigeria through local chiefs and emirs whose lands naturally split the country into north, east and west. The divides were still there when Nigeria became independent in 1960 and have caused many conflicts ever since. The most serious of these followed the discovery of oil near Port Harcourt in eastern Nigeria. The Igbo people living there wanted independence from Nigeria and from 1967 to 1970 fought a violent civil war over the region called Biafra. Over one million Nigerians died as a result. As Nigeria struggles to unite its people, the war is a reminder of their divided past and of the need for peace and stability today.

▲ *The emir's palace in Kano. The emirs continue to have a strong influence and are greatly respected by local people.*

IN THEIR OWN WORDS

'My name is Essiet U Essiet and I was an officer during the Biafra civil war between 1967 and 1970. I fought for the Biafran side, but it was hard to fight against our Nigerian brothers and sisters. The war was over oil and who would control it. After the war, it didn't take long for our people to come together again. I moved to the north of the country to start a new life and I'm now a university professor. There are still disputes among our ethnic groups, but nobody wants another Biafra. To build a strong country, we must work together and put our differences behind us. For example, my three children now speak Hausa, as well as our own language, Igbo.'

3 Landscape and Climate

Nigeria is the fourteenth biggest country in Africa, covering an area of 923,768 sq km, close to three and half times bigger than the UK. Nigeria is bordered by Niger and Chad to the north, Cameroon to the east and Benin to the west. Its southern border is a coastal strip of 853 km on the Gulf of Guinea, part of the Atlantic Ocean. Nigeria's landscape and climate are extremely varied, but can be divided into three main bands that run across the north, the middle and the south of the country.

▲ *This sand dune is being stabilized by planting trees along its ridge. Such methods help to reduce and may even reverse desertification.*

The dry north

The north of Nigeria is the driest region of the country. Annual rainfall can be less than 400 mm in the far north with the main rainy season being May to September. The north is also very hot and daytime temperatures can reach 38 °C. The landscape is mainly flat with large plains that stretch northwards into the Sahel region and the Sahara desert beyond. In much of the north agriculture is only possible where the land is artificially

◄ *The dry plains outside of Maiduguri in northern Nigeria burst into life following the arrival of the rains.*

watered or close to major sources of water such as the Hadejia-Nguru wetlands. Many people keep livestock, travelling long distances as they follow the rains in search of fresh pasture. A feature of the north is a dusty dry wind called the 'Harmattan' which blows off the Sahara desert towards the coast between November and January.

◀ *The dust carried by the Harmattan can turn day into dusk, but it also deposits valuable nutrients on the farmers' fields.*

IN THEIR OWN WORDS

'My name is Biliyamin and I am a climatologist at Bayero University in Kano. My job is to monitor weather conditions and try to find trends and patterns. This part of the country is very dry, and one of the main concerns in this region is the threat of desertification. This is when the land is turned into desert as a result of climate changes, but also because of human activities such as deforestation or overgrazing. Today, many believe that desertification can be reversed and that the land can recover with time. Whether this is true or not the climate plays a key role in the process. It remains as important as ever to keep track of climatic change.'

The 'Middle Belt'

Across the centre of Nigeria lie the plateaux of the Middle Belt. These are upland regions of high plains and wide valleys. Occasional mountains are also found in the Middle Belt, including Nigeria's highest peak, Mt Dimlang (2,042 m) on the Cameroon border. The Jos Plateau rises in the centre of the Middle Belt and has a cooler climate that makes it ideal for intensive dairy farming. Throughout the rest of the Middle Belt farming is a major activity. Crops such as sorghum, millet, maize, cowpeas and sesame seed are among the most important. Rice and tea are also grown in some areas. Nigeria's two main rivers, the Niger and the Benue, meet on the southern edge of the Middle Belt before flowing south to the coast.

▼ *The Niger river on the edge of the Middle Belt. It is important for local people as a transport route and a source of water and fish and for industries such as the paper mill in the background.*

IN THEIR OWN WORDS

'I'm Rabiu and I'm 15 years old. I'm a Fulani pastoralist from northern Nigeria. During the dry season we migrate to the Middle Belt or the south in search of fresh pastures for our cattle. We return to the north with the rains. This lifestyle is becoming more difficult because more and more land is being used by farmers to meet the food needs of our growing population. This means there is less pasture available and our cattle routes can be severely disrupted. As a result many Fulani have had to reduce their herd size and some have even become part-time farmers. I know that I might have to change, but I hope to keep herding cattle as my father taught me.'

The humid south

The south, like the north, is dominated by flat plains. The climate is more humid here with high rainfall of up to 3,000 mm per year in the far south-east and around 1,800 mm per year in the south-west. Temperatures are more constant along the coast and range from 21 °C to 33 °C throughout the year. Tropical rainforests thrive in the hot, wet conditions of the south and once covered much of the region. Today they are under threat from human activities such as farming, industry and urban growth. The coast is lined with mangrove swamps (themselves a type of rainforest) and is dominated by the giant Niger delta where the river ends its life and deposits its rich sediment load.

▼ *Rainforests in Nigeria grow where the climate is warm and rainfall plentiful. However, human use of the forests means they are shrinking .*

4 Natural Resources

Black gold!

Unlike many of its African neighbours, Nigeria is a country rich in natural resources. Many of these are of great importance to the economy. The most important of Nigeria's natural resources is its oil or 'black gold' as it is sometimes known. In 2002 Nigeria was the world's tenth biggest oil producer. Most of the oil is found in the Niger delta region around Port Harcourt, but new reserves are now under development in the Gulf of Guinea too. By 2010 these new deepwater reserves are expected to double Nigeria's oil production to around 4 million barrels per day. Nigeria's oil is very important to the economy and accounts for around 95 per cent of its foreign exchange earnings. Unfortunately much of this money is misspent due to corruption by the government and oil companies. The challenge for the future is to make this natural wealth benefit everyone in Nigeria and not just a privileged few.

▲ *Drilling for oil in the Niger delta. Without oil, Nigeria would be a much poorer country.*

Energy resources

Most of Nigeria's oil is exported, leaving relatively little for local use. In fact Nigeria imports refined oil products to meet its energy needs because it has too few refineries of its own. Many people still depend on biomass fuels such as wood and charcoal for their energy and only 40 per cent of the population have access to electricity. Even where electricity is

IN THEIR OWN WORDS

'My name is Azu Misha, and I'm the superintendent here at Kurra Falls Hydro Electric Development Project on the Jos Plateau. Although we are only a medium-sized power station we generate electricity for thousands of households on the plateau and neighbouring Kaduna state. We also supply power for many important industries in the town of Jos. Using water to generate electricity (hydroelectric power (HEP)) is an important source of energy for Nigeria. It is much cleaner than using fossil fuels such as oil. As demand for electricity continues to grow in Nigeria I believe that HEP will play an important role in meeting our country's needs. Here at Kurra Falls we are already looking for ways to expand the project.'

available the supply is very unreliable and power cuts lasting three or four days are not unusual. Around 47 per cent of electricity is generated from hydroelectric power (HEP). The Kainji Dam project on the Niger river is the biggest and most important in the country.

▼ *A wood fuel cutter in Kano chops logs that have been brought in from rural areas. He will sell them to provide urban residents with fuel.*

Mineral reserves

Besides oil, Nigeria has several other mineral resources. Coal is found in large quantities and is among the cleanest burning varieties in the world. This makes it very attractive to countries that use coal as an energy source. Nigeria is now developing its coal industry to meet this demand. Tin, iron ore, limestone and columbite are among Nigeria's other important minerals. Limestone is used to make cement for the construction industry and iron ore is used in the manufacture of steel. Tin mining was once a major industry on the Jos Plateau, but has declined as aluminium has replaced many of the uses for tin. Columbite contains a metal called niobium that is used in the manufacture of electromagnets and some types of stainless steel. Small amounts of gold, gemstones and uranium are also found.

▲ *A tin miner with the finished tin ore. The ore is mined using a high pressure hose to blast the cliffs in the background.*

Forests

Nigeria's forests once covered large areas of the country. Today they cover only around 10 per cent of the total land area. Forest products are widely used by around 90 per cent of the rural population for fuel wood, food products, timber, construction materials and local medicines. Population growth and rising oil-

◀ *A sawmill in Benin City processes tropical timber. The best wood will be exported, but lower-quality timber is used locally.*

◀ *A tree nursery in Jigawa state. Tree planting is promoted by the government to reduce problems such as soil erosion.*

fuel prices have placed great pressure on the forests as people turn to wood as an alternative fuel. Experts believe that if current rates of deforestation continue then all of Nigeria's forests could be gone by 2020. The government is now launching various action plans to protect and conserve the forests. It is also encouraging tree planting and hopes to increase forest cover to 25 per cent of Nigeria by 2010.

IN THEIR OWN WORDS

'I'm Gabriel and I work as a conservation officer here at Okomu National Park in Edo State. At one time, this area was covered in thick forest, but today our park contains the last rainforests in southwest Nigeria. It is a very important park and is home to many endangered species, like the White-Throat monkey. We use this 'tree house' observation station for research and to monitor poaching by local people who use the forest to hunt for bush meat. We realize that people depend on the forest for their livelihoods and should not be cut off completely, but it is in everyone's interest to manage the forest wisely. Finding the balance between local needs and conservation remains a great challenge!'

5 The Changing Environment

The management of the environment is one of Nigeria's greatest challenges. In many rural areas, deforestation, overgrazing and soil erosion are serious problems. In urban areas, water supplies, sanitation, waste disposal and pollution are among the biggest concerns. Not everything is bad news however. There are also examples from across Nigeria of positive efforts to protect and conserve the environment for future generations.

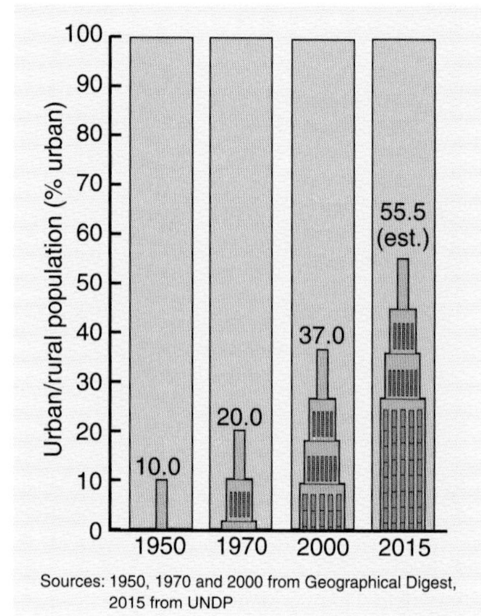

▲ *Less than half the population of Nigeria lives in towns and cities now. That will change dramatically over the next few years.*

◀ *This view of housing in Kano shows the high density of urban settlement typical of many Nigerian towns.*

Urban decay

At independence in 1960, a little over 10 per cent of Nigeria's 42 million people lived in urban areas. During British colonial rule, laws had prevented people from moving to urban areas, but these were lifted at independence and Nigeria's urban centres began to grow at an alarming rate. By 2000, almost 40 per cent of Nigerians lived in urban areas, an incredible 49 million people or more than the entire population at independence!

▼ *Brick makers work hard to keep up with the demand for building materials in Nigeria's expanding urban centres.*

Nigeria's urban areas have been unable to cope with such growth. The lack of housing means that people have been forced to build houses out of whatever materials they can find. Large shanty towns have developed close to many urban centres. Services such as electricity and sewage disposal are also lacking. For example, only 58 per cent of urban residents have access to a safe water supply. Urban roads are congested and poorly maintained vehicles create a choking haze of pollution. The burning of waste adds to urban pollution because very little waste is collected. Plastic bags are a particular problem. They can clog drains and create stagnant pools that encourage the spread of diseases such as typhoid and malaria.

▼ *With few collection schemes, urban waste can build up very rapidly.*

IN THEIR OWN WORDS

'My name is Peter Omokhudu and I'm 19 years old. I've lived in Lagos my entire life, and for the past few years I've been working as a water seller. Water selling is a good business because so many houses here do not have a piped water supply. For instance, there is no water flowing through the pipes on this entire street. People must get their water from another source. I fill jerry cans from a bore hole, and push my cart down the street. By the time I reach the end, I will have sold all the water. It's too bad that the water supply is so poor, but I feel that I am providing a useful service, and I have created a job for myself too!'

Greening the cities

With Nigeria's urban population still growing at between 5 and 10 per cent a year the natural environment surrounding urban areas is now under serious threat. Resources such as fuel wood, food and even water are increasingly being brought in from rural areas. Around Kano for example wood is brought into the city by donkey from up to 20 kilometres away. This not only leads to further environmental destruction, but also makes things very expensive. In many cities, for example, food alone can take up over half of people's incomes.

◀ *Fuel wood is one of many resources transported from rural areas to urban centres.*

In many Nigerian towns and cities residents cope with this problem by greening the cities with urban farms. Almost any small plot of land is turned into a productive farm growing many of the staple crops that local people eat. Any surplus crops are sold in local markets to earn extra income. Urban farms have led to other positive schemes too. For example, in some places waste is now sorted into organic and non-organic matter. The organic waste can then be used as a fertilizer on urban farms. This process also takes place beyond urban areas with waste being transported to rural areas to be sorted for the same purpose. One disadvantage is that this has caused higher levels of non-organic waste in rural areas such as plastic bags, which can block rural waterways.

▲ *This farmer is sorting through urban waste. He will separate out the organic content and use it as a manure for his fields.*

Other recycling projects are also helping to green the cities. In 1995 for example, local entrepreneurs began manufacturing toilet paper from recycled paper. This has helped to establish a paper recycling industry in Nigeria and reduced the need to import toilet paper. Plastic bags are also being recycled and used to make items such as plastic wash bowls and cups. A common form of footwear, the 'flip-flop', is also recycled to make new ones. Children can be seen collecting old flip-flops and returning them to the factories for a small payment.

IN THEIR OWN WORDS

'My name is Elizabeth Obi and I live in Ogoja, Cross River State. Living in the city is more difficult today. Unemployment is high and the cost of food is high. Most people cannot grow food in urban places, but I am lucky. I have this farm plot behind the secondary school. Right now I am transplanting cassava stalks, which will be ready in May. We will eat yams until then. Cassava is a good crop because it grows very easily, and almost anywhere – even in the city! I am thankful for my urban farm. The food we grow helps my family to make ends meet. There are other unused plots nearby. More people should be encouraged to become urban farmers like me!'

Dirty business

One of Nigeria's most severe environmental problems is pollution from the oil industry. In the Niger delta region wetlands and farmland have been damaged or destroyed by pollution from the oil industry. Fish stocks in local rivers have also declined due to oil pollution, ruining local livelihoods. Between 1976 and 1996 an incredible 2.4 million barrels of oil spilt into the Niger delta from leaking pipelines. In 2001, the government demanded that oil companies must reduce the risk of pollution from their pipelines.

◀ *Most rural families depend on wells for their water supply. They frequently dry up during the dry season and must be dug deeper.*

Land pressures

Despite the increase in urban populations the majority of Nigerians still live in rural areas. A lack of services means that rural people depend on the environment for their basic needs such as fuel wood, water and food. As the population has grown it is placing greater pressure on the ability of the land to support so many people. The removal of trees has led to an increase in soil erosion and this in turn has led to declining crop yields in some regions. Farmers use techniques such as terracing to try to reduce soil erosion from their land. Tree planting schemes also reduce erosion and provide a local

◀ *Gully erosion is a major problem in Nigeria. The soils become weak and vulnerable to erosion by wind and rain when the vegetation is cleared by people and their livestock.*

source of fuel wood. The government promotes the use of fuel-efficient stoves to reduce the burning of wood and charcoal. They are also promoting alternative energy sources such as solar power or biogas from vegetable and animal waste. By working with local people, such schemes can prevent or reverse environmental losses, but the challenge remains significant.

IN THEIR OWN WORDS

'I'm Amina Karkarna and I'm a nursery attendant for the Ministry of the Environment in Jigawa State. Behind me, you can see one of our shelterbelt projects which has been very beneficial for local farmers. A shelterbelt is a strip of trees about 30 metres across, planted in a long row. The trees act as a barrier to the wind, and so help to reduce soil erosion on the farms alongside. We are also planting 'multiple use' shelterbelts that in addition to controlling erosion also act as a fuel wood reserve. By careful harvesting the shelterbelt can meet the local demand for fuel wood. It is important to take people's needs into consideration if projects to protect the environment are to work and be sustainable.'

6 The Changing Population

The Giant of Africa

Of the 606 million people living in sub-Saharan Africa in 2000, almost one in every five (19 per cent) is Nigerian! When it comes to population, Nigeria is the giant of Africa and the tenth most populous nation in the world. It is also among the fastest growing populations in the world at an average rate of 2.9 per cent per year. If current trends continue, the population will reach 165 million by 2015 and more than double to 244 million by 2050. Such rapid growth is partly explained by the fact that almost half the population is under the age of 15 and yet to start their own families. But poverty is also a major factor.

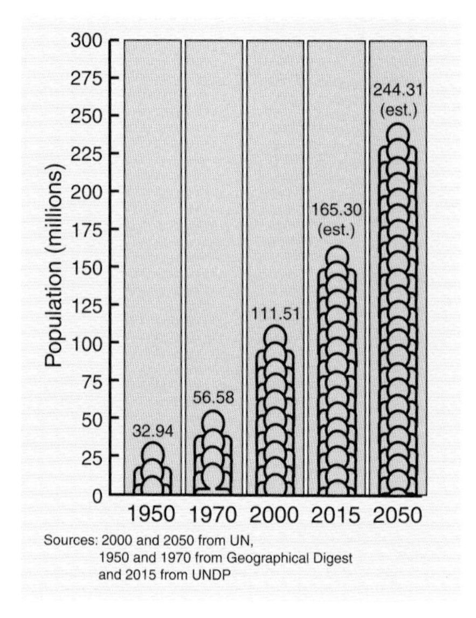

▲ *Unlike many developed countries where the population has stabilized or may even be declining, Nigeria's population is predicted to more than double by the middle of the twenty-first century.*

◀ *Nigeria's youthful population presents a major challenge for the government to provide facilities such as schooling and healthcare.*

Poor families often can't afford the healthcare necessary to give children a healthy start in life. As a result the number of children who die in infancy (up to 5 years of age) is extremely high at around 18 per cent. Because of this people often choose to have many children in order to ensure that some will survive. As healthcare in Nigeria has improved, child mortality has fallen from 204 per 1,000 live births in 1960 to the current level of 184 per 1,000. With more children surviving the population has grown rapidly. This growth is even greater because women continue to have an average of 6 children each, only slightly down from 7 in 1970.

◀ *The cost of basic healthcare means that these young boys have only a one in five chance of surviving to celebrate their fifth birthday.*

IN THEIR OWN WORDS

'My name is Ibrahim and this is my extended family. Actually, it is only part of my family. We number over 100 people in this compound! These are some of my brothers, sisters and cousins with their children. Extended families are important in Nigeria, because unlike some countries we cannot rely on government support when times are difficult. Instead, we must help one another. The more fortunate of us are expected to assist those most in need. Each month I contribute part of my salary to the greater good of the family. Extended families have long been part of my culture, and I can't see this changing in the future. More than ever, we must stick together.'

Population choice

In the mid-1980s the government realized that it must do something to slow population growth. If it didn't act then it would become increasingly difficult to provide basic services such as health and education. In 1988 new policies were introduced to make family planning services such as contraception and reproductive advice more widely available. Use of family planning services tripled, but was still only being used by around 15 per cent of married women in 2000. A lack of health centres, the costs involved, and a reluctance by some to use new methods, are the reasons for its limited success. Giving people the choice and ability to plan their families remains one of the government's urgent tasks.

▼ *Improving the availability of family planning choices to young women is a central aim of Nigeria's population policy.*

IN THEIR OWN WORDS

'I'm Dr Binta and I work at this rural clinic in Port Harcourt. This mother has come in for a check-up for herself and her baby. We see many, many patients every day. In fact one of our main problems is that we are understaffed, we can't meet the demand. Medicines are expensive for most of our patients and so we focus our efforts on sickness prevention through health education. We teach local communities about nutrition, sanitation, and HIV/AIDS prevention. This way people can avoid becoming sick. Poverty is a cause of much ill health, so poverty alleviation is necessary for a strong and healthy country. A healthy and educated population is vital to meet the challenges that lie ahead for Nigeria.'

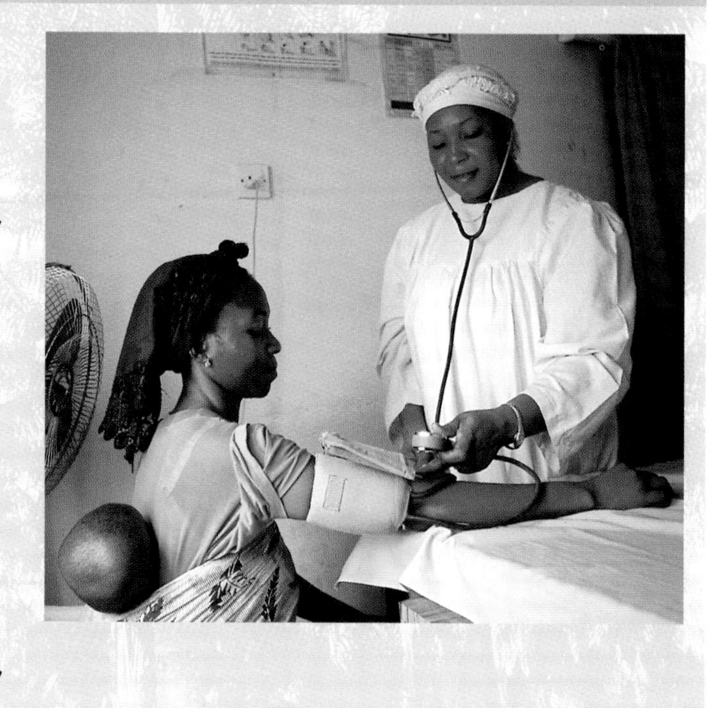

Ethnic divides

Besides its size the other characteristic of the Nigerian population is its extraordinary mix of ethnic groups. In total there are over 350 ethnic groups who between them speak at least 450 languages! Such diversity makes Nigeria a fascinating country, but has also been the cause of many of its problems. Different ethnic groups have not always been in agreement with one another and at times this has led to violent conflicts. The main groups involved in these tensions are the Hausa-Fulani, the Yoruba and the Igbo people. Together they make up nearly 70 per cent of the population and have dominated Nigerian politics since independence in 1960. Today ethnic relations are relatively quiet, but as in the past, tension could erupt again with little warning.

▼ *Markets and trading provide a common link between Nigeria's many different ethnic groups.*

7 Changes at Home

Family life

Family life in Nigeria varies considerably depending on where people live. There are strong divides between the northern Islamic states and the southern Christian ones for example. Under Islamic culture it is permitted for a man to have up to four wives (a system known as polygamy) and so families can be extremely large. In Christian areas, polygamy is less common, but families are still large, especially in rural areas. Having a large family in rural areas is of great benefit because it means there is plentiful supply of labour. Children may start working around the home from as young as 5 or 6. By the age of 12 they may be contributing as much to the household as their parents do.

◀ *Young children regularly help with farming and household activities. This girl is weeding her mother's field.*

In rural areas families often live together in a family compound. It is normal for families to stay living together as they grow older, even when they start their own families. In parts of northern Nigeria up to one hundred members of an extended family may live in the same compound. In urban areas, families tend to be smaller, but are still large by African standards. Children are considered as a sign of wealth and

IN THEIR OWN WORDS

'I'm Halima (on the left) and this is Nana. We are from Kano city in the north of Nigeria which is an Islamic area. According to our beliefs, it is possible for a man to marry more than one wife. We are both married to the same man, an arrangement that works well for us both. We have many children in our family, but with two of us it is possible to share the work load. If one of us falls sick, the other can continue caring for the family. Of course sharing the same husband can be challenging, but our husband tries to treat us equally. The key to making our family work is good communication so that we can avoid any misunderstandings!'

prestige by many Nigerians and so large families remain important. Although average family sizes have decreased a little since the 1970s, large families are likely to remain part of Nigerian life for the foreseeable future.

▼ *The value of families and especially children means families are very large across most of Nigeria.*

Women's roles

The role of women varies greatly between the north and south of Nigeria. This is because the Islamic culture of the north demands a more secluded life for women. A practice called 'purdah' means that married women of child-bearing age must stay within the family compound. They are not encouraged to work in the fields or conduct their business in public. However, many do have businesses and use their children to help them run errands and trade goods. This important role for many women is carried out alongside caring for their children and the household, tasks that are often shared with their co-wives. Secluded women also work hard to process crops from the fields – drying and shelling maize or husking rice. They also carry out the labour-intensive tasks of food processing and food preparation.

◀ *This young girl is being prepared for a life of purdah from an early age. Here she is wearing a hijab, part of typical Islamic dress, which has become fashionable in recent years.*

IN THEIR OWN WORDS

'This is Mariama and I'm Aisha (right) and we live in Kaduna state. We are taking part in a Skills Acquisition Program where we are being taught to sew on a six-month course. Sewing can earn women a good income in this part of the country. When we graduate from our training, we can keep the sewing machines to help us to get started in business. We have one year to pay back this loan, but it should not be difficult. Micro-credit schemes such as this are very good, especially for women because we are sometimes excluded from development initiatives. After we have paid the loan the income we earn will benefit our entire families, and help us in the upkeep of our households.'

In southern Nigeria, women are far more visible in public. Like women in the north they not only look after their children and the household, but also earn an income for their family. This is often known as the 'triple burden' of women and can be very time consuming. Women often work much longer hours than men and have a busy life as they balance their different roles. The government recognizes the important role women play in Nigeria and supports numerous schemes designed to help women. Some involve teaching them new skills or providing small loans so that women can develop their own businesses. The income women earn benefits the whole family, and helps to lift them out of poverty. Women still remain much poorer than men however, earning less than half their income on average.

▼ *This woman is washing clothes and dishes in the Niger river. Such jobs are just one of the many burdens women have.*

Education

Education in Nigeria involves six years of primary school and two three-year periods of secondary education. Although education is free, additional costs such as uniforms, books and lunches mean that many parents can't afford to educate their children. Others may begin their schooling but fail to complete it for financial or other reasons. In fact, in 2000 over 20 per cent of primary school children in Nigeria dropped out before completing their studies. Some drop out because they are expected to work for their families, especially in rural areas. Cultural beliefs that place a low value on education also lead to high drop-out rates. This is especially true in the north where Nigeria's Western-style education system is considered to clash with Islamic cultural values. Across the country girls are more likely to be withdrawn from school than boys. This is because they are normally married at a younger age than young men and so education is often considered to be wasted on them.

▼ *Nigeria has a large university population compared to many African countries.*

An unusual feature of northern Nigeria is its many religious schools. These were around long before Western education was introduced during the colonial period. They teach according to Islamic culture and beliefs. Some of their students continue their education at Islamic universities in countries such as Saudi Arabia. Nigeria also has over 50 secular universities and polytechnics. Courses in science, engineering and business management are among the most popular and run for four years on average. Nigeria produces around 70,000 graduates every year.

▲ *These girls are working at home instead of attending school.*

IN THEIR OWN WORDS

'My name is Abdullahi Zakari and I am a junior secondary school student in Jigawa state. I am very happy to be attending school because there are many children in Nigeria that are not able to receive an education. For example, my sisters are not going to school because soon they will be married and will be expected to stay at home. One of the main problems in educating children is that it is very expensive for most families. But in our state, the government has encouraged community involvement in the running of schools. This not only cuts costs but it makes our community feel good too. Schools like mine would not have opened without the help of the community, and I am very grateful for the chance to attend school.'

Diet

Because of its varied climate the foods that are traditionally grown and eaten across Nigeria vary considerably. In the north the staple foods include millet, sorghum, groundnuts and cowpeas, whilst in the south yams, cassava and other root crops are more common. Nearly all Nigerian meals are based around a serving of the local staple together with a sauce or stew that is normally referred to as soup. One of the main foods in urban areas is bread, but this was only introduced during the colonial period. Most of the wheat used to make bread is imported and this makes it a relatively expensive food compared with more traditional staples.

▲ *Tuwo is the staple food in northern Nigeria and is normally served with a spicy sauce or 'soup'.*

Food production

The majority of Nigerians grow their own food, but need to purchase inputs such as fertilizers and seeds. In recent years, changes in government policies and a cut in funding for agriculture have made it harder and more expensive to buy such inputs. In addition new trade policies mean that cheap

▲ *A bread seller in Benin City. Bread has become a staple food, especially in urban areas.*

grains from countries such as the USA are now available in Nigeria. This has reduced the demand for locally produced food and led some people to give up farming altogether. Nigeria today imports more food than it exports and will have to revive its agricultural sector if it is to meet the needs of its growing population.

◀ *These children are cooking kosai – a doughnut-type snack made from beans popular throughout Nigeria.*

IN THEIR OWN WORDS

'Hello, we are Sarah, Zara and Faith and we're selling Irish potatoes at this market on the Jos Plateau. Today, many Nigerians enjoy our crop, but potatoes were not historically part of our diet. They were introduced by the British during the period of colonial rule, but have now become a staple part of the diet for many Nigerians. The Plateau region with its mild climate, higher elevation, and rich dark soil has the perfect growing conditions for potatoes. Many farmers now choose to grow them and although it is hard work, we can get good prices for them. In fact potatoes from here are transported and sold in markets all over Nigeria.'

Health and medicine

Nigeria's main health problems are closely related to the poor living conditions suffered by much of its population. For example, a lack of clean water and poor sanitation are the cause of many water-borne diseases such as cholera, typhoid and hepatitis. Diarrhoea is also related to poor sanitation and is one of the biggest killers of children in Nigeria. It is easily avoided by educating people about basic hygiene or treated using oral rehydration therapy (ORT) – a simple solution of salts and sugar. Between 1994 and 2000 however, less than a quarter of infants with diarrhoea were treated using ORT. Nigerian health facilities are reasonably good for Africa, but

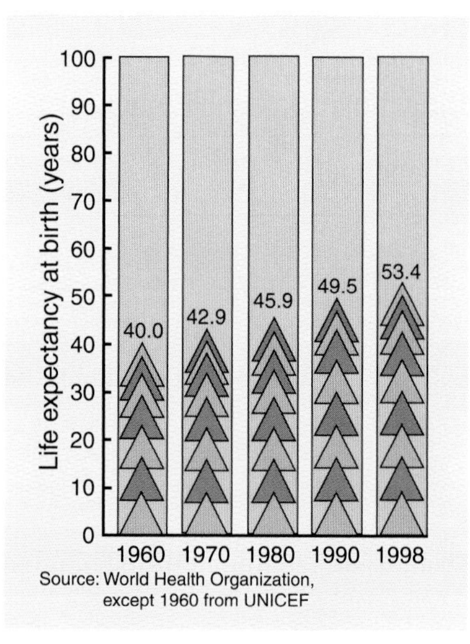

▲ *From 1960 to 1998, the age to which Nigerians could expect to live has increased but there is still plenty of room for improvement.*

◀ *Unofficial drug sellers are a common sight on Nigerian streets, but relatively few of them have any proper medical training.*

IN THEIR OWN WORDS

'I'm Sister Catherine and I'm the headmistress of a girls' college in Kano. We're a Catholic church, and in addition to running a school, we're involved in community development projects to reduce poverty. It is challenging being a Christian in Kano. The State is governed by Islamic law and in recent years there has been tension between Christians and Muslims here. There have been frequent street riots and shops have been looted. People blame the tension on religion, but there are more serious problems under the surface, like poverty, unemployment and lack of education. Many uneducated street youths look for excuses to cause problems if they can benefit. Ultimately, regardless of our religion, we are all human beings and should live together happily and peacefully!'

there are still only 18 doctors for every 100,000 people. The introduction of user fees after 1986 has led many people to turn to cheaper local healers as an alternative. Unfortunately this has encouraged some people to set up as false healers and take advantage of the sick. Trained healers and village health workers are valuable in meeting Nigeria's healthcare needs though, especially for the poor.

A religious split

Perhaps the biggest divide in Nigeria is along religious grounds. The Muslim north has recently adopted Islamic (Sharia) law in many states and is governed by strict Islamic beliefs. The Christian south is a more Westernized society, having been influenced by missionary activity during the colonial period. Tensions between these two different societies frequently turn into localized conflicts. Overcoming their differences is vital to creating a more stable and united Nigeria.

▼ This channel is being tested for water quality. One of the most common pollutants is human sewage.

8 Changes at Work

Agricultural economy

Despite the dominance of oil in Nigeria, it remains a mainly agricultural economy. Around 40 per cent of Nigeria's workforce is occupied in the agricultural sector and agriculture accounts for 40 per cent of the country's income (GDP). Much of the agriculture in Nigeria is subsistence farming whereby families grow food for their own consumption and sell any surplus supplies in local and national markets. Commercial farming is limited to a relatively small number of extremely large farms and plantations. Groundnuts and palm oil are two commercial crops (sometimes called 'cash crops') that have been grown in Nigeria since colonial times. Cocoa, cotton and rubber are among other cash crops grown in Nigeria, both on plantations and by subsistence farmers who sell them to provide an income.

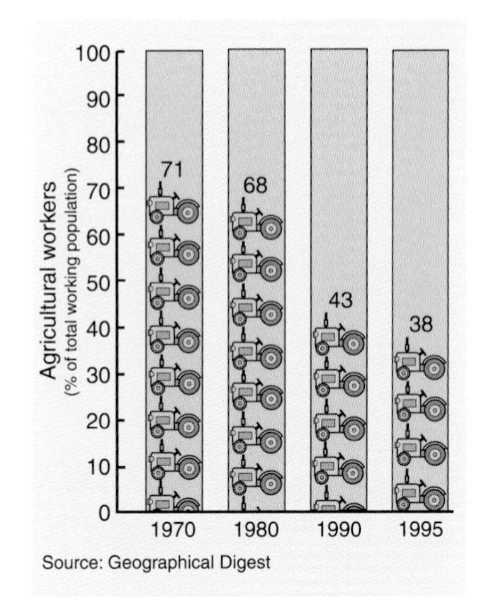

▲ *The proportion of people working in agriculture as a percentage of the total working population almost halved from 1970 to 1995.*

◀ *Palm-oil plantations such as this one were first established during the colonial period – they remain a major cash crop today.*

The central plateau region of Nigeria is ideally suited to dairy cows and supports a significant dairy industry. Livestock including cattle, goats and sheep are kept by Nigeria's pastoral people and their milk, meat and hides are exchanged for other goods and services. Across Nigeria, agriculture suffers from a lack of government investment and increased pressure on scarce land resources. Pastoral communities are especially affected. Expanding urban areas, new dams and reservoirs, and commercial farms interfere with traditional pastoral routes. As they seek alternatives, pastoralists are brought into conflict with settled farmers over the use of the land and watering holes for their animals.

◀ *Pastoralists must keep close guard of their cattle to prevent them eating or damaging farmers' crops.*

IN THEIR OWN WORDS

'My name is Mustapha Lawal. I work for the West African Milk Corporation in Vom, Plateau State. The plateau has a mild climate and fertile land that makes it perfect for dairy cows, but the industry was traditionally very hard work. During the 1980s, our company realized that to compete in a changing world, modern production and technical expertise were needed. Today, we are half owned by the Dutch, who are world experts in the dairy business. We have increased our milk output by crossbreeding local animals with species from Holland. We have also introduced new mechanical milking technology. We today control half of the dairy market in Nigeria. Our success lies in keeping up with current production methods and our partnership with the Dutch ensures we have the leading dairy technology from Europe.'

Changing industry

Industry employs just 10 per cent of Nigeria's workforce, but its high value products contribute about 40 per cent to the country's GDP – the same as agriculture. Because of its high value to the economy, industry receives much more funding than other sectors of the economy. The oil industry is the most valuable single industry accounting for around 20 per cent of GDP, but coal mining and other mineral-extraction industries are also important. Manufacturing in Nigeria is still fairly minor, but various goods are produced including chemicals, textiles and steel products. Nigeria also manufactures motor vehicles including cars for the French company Peugeot. But poor standards and an increase in imports of cheap second-hand vehicles (many of which are imported illegally from neighbouring Benin) have seen Nigeria's vehicle industry virtually collapse in recent years. Like much of manufacturing the vehicle industry is in urgent need of investment if it is to remain competitive.

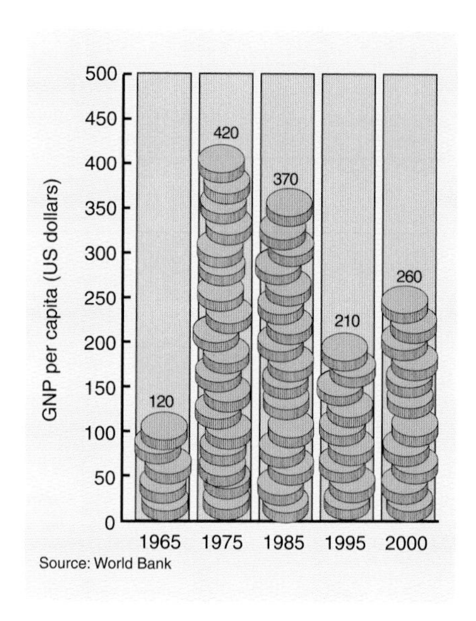

▲ *The average GNP (Gross National Product) for each Nigerian person fluctuated greatly between 1965 and 2000.*

◀ *Making improvements to Nigeria's railway network might help encourage investors to set up businesses in the country.*

There is great potential for manufacturing in Nigeria because of its enormous domestic market of over 110 million people and its strong trading links within Africa and beyond. The key is providing the political stability that will encourage overseas investors to set up their businesses in Nigeria. Many of the British who originally stayed at independence have since left, but more recent business entrepreneurs from China, Lebanon and India are now present in Nigeria. To encourage further international investment, Nigeria must improve its transport and telecommunications networks to provide people with the tools to do business.

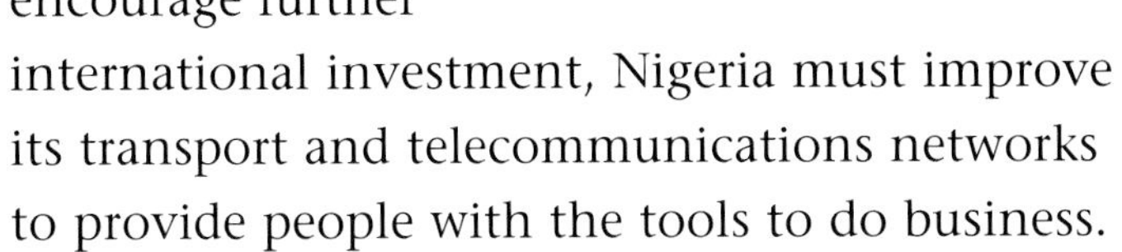

▲ *Improving basic communications is vital to the future growth of the economy. Very few Nigerians have access to a telephone.*

IN THEIR OWN WORDS

'My name is Loretta and I sell mobile telephones in Abuja. The mobile industry is new to Nigeria. Many people are just realizing how convenient cell phones can be. For many it is the first time they've had any telephone at all, since most Nigerians don't have land lines due to their high cost and unreliability. Mobile phones are also relatively expensive, but in time the price will come down. Of course, some people would argue that Nigerians should concentrate on more basic problems before we worry about mobile phones. But having access to knowledge and information is an important part of development. In this age of information technology, it is important for Nigeria to keep up with the rest of the world!'

The informal economy

Nigeria's service sector is relatively small and accounts for around 20 per cent of both the workforce and GDP. This is partly because Nigeria's poverty means the demand for services such as banking, insurance and travel is limited. But it is also explained by the extremely active informal economy. The informal economy offers many of the same services that can be found in the formal economy such as market traders, mechanics, welders, carpenters, drivers and hairdressers. The difference is that the income earned in the informal economy is not taxed or regulated by the government. This means that it can cost the government a great deal of money in lost tax revenue. On the positive side however, the informal economy has brought many goods and services within reach of Nigeria's poorest communities. The informal economy also acts as a training ground for skills that can be transferred into the formal economy. For this reason the informal economy, which may account for 45 per cent of Nigeria's GDP, is largely tolerated by government.

▼ This man working at the dye-pits in Kano is part of Nigeria's informal economy, providing a valuable service to local people.

◀ *Barbed wire fences help to protect wealthy homes such as this from robberies. Crime is a problem caused by inequalities between the rich and poor.*

Employment and crime

One of Nigeria's greatest challenges is to generate greater employment opportunities for its massive and youthful population. The formal unemployment rate is very high at around 28 per cent. With few opportunities to earn a stable and regular income, many of Nigeria's youth turn to crime as they become desperate for a better life. Crime rates in Nigeria's main cities are particularly high as there is a concentration of wealth and poverty in a single location.

IN THEIR OWN WORDS

'My name is Vincent Emeka and I'm from Enugu. For the past seven years, I've been selling second-hand shoes in the market here. Once a month, I travel by bus to Cotonou in neighbouring Benin. I buy up to 100 pairs of shoes from an importer who ships used shoes in from Europe and America. Shoes are cheaper in Benin so I can make a profit selling them back in Nigeria. If business is good I can make a lot of money selling shoes, especially around Christmas when I might sell ten pairs in a day. My shoes are high quality, especially after I have reconditioned them. With our poor economy, most people cannot afford new shoes, so I am providing a valuable service.'

A national resource

One of Nigeria's greatest resources is its people. Its labour force is among the most highly educated and skilled in Africa. There is also a wealth of traditional skills and crafts in Nigeria that could be better utilized for the benefit of the whole economy. One of Nigeria's problems however is that it offers relatively few opportunities for people to invest in and develop their skills. Many of the most educated and skilled people become frustrated and end up leaving Nigeria in search of opportunities abroad. This leads to what is known as a 'brain drain' and further undermines Nigeria's ability to develop its workforce and economy. It is not all bad news though. Every year an estimated 2,000 Nigerians return to the country having worked or been educated abroad. They bring with them new skills, ideas and contacts – all important for leading Nigeria's economy into the twenty-first century.

▼ President Olusegun Obasanjo is working hard to provide a better future for the people and economy of Nigeria and its neighbours.

◀ *Due to corruption in the oil industry, a lot of Nigeria's oil is sold on the black market both within the country and in neighbouring states.*

Government support

The government is working to improve the opportunities for Nigeria's workforce. One of its key objectives is to reduce corruption in order to encourage foreign investment in Nigeria. In 1999 Nigeria was judged as the most corrupt country in the world, a reputation that is extremely damaging to business and industry. But in the same year, President Obasanjo introduced tough new anti-corruption laws to try to reverse Nigeria's corruption problem. The future of much of Nigeria's workforce will depend on how effective the new laws prove to be and on how quickly foreign companies are prepared to invest in Nigeria and its people.

IN THEIR OWN WORDS

'I'm Hauwa'u and I'm a Yoruba woman from near Ibadan. I've been making clay pots my whole life. In my culture, pot making is an activity that is carried out exclusively by women. First, we travel to the outskirts of the city to dig the clay; it is very hard work. Then, we mould the clay into pots and bake them in a very hot fire. You can see some of the finished pots behind me. Our pots are very popular because they are good for keeping water cool. Traditionally, pot making has been an important industry for women. We control the entire business, and the money we earn from selling them is important for the well being of our families.'

9 The Way Ahead

A new era

In May 1999 Olusegun Obasanjo was elected as Nigeria's civilian president and ushered in a new era of hope for the future of his country. Of Nigeria's first 40 years of independence (1960–2000), 29 were spent under military rule – a lasting reminder of the country's complex and unstable past. At the start of the twenty-first century though, there is a mood of optimism among Nigeria's people. They have had enough of ethnic and religious tensions, enough of military leaders, and enough of the corruption that benefits an élite few but keeps millions of Nigerians in poverty.

◀ *Technology such as the Internet may present Nigeria's future generation with new opportunities to succeed in the global economy.*

IN THEIR OWN WORDS

'My name is Wumi and I'm a 19-year-old student at the University of Ilorin in Kwara State. I've just started my Bachelor's Degree in Education, and in a few years, I will qualify as a teacher. One of the reasons that I have chosen to be a teacher is that I believe education is the key to a strong future for Nigeria. Not only will teaching provide me with a steady income, but I will be playing a role in developing my country too. Nigeria will not be truly self-sufficient until we can keep up in a fast-changing world. Today, modern technology and advances in communication are changing things very fast. More than ever before, we must face the future together as an educated population.'

The first few years of Obasanjo's rule have been promising. Laws have been passed to reduce corruption and promote foreign investment. Businesses are returning to Nigeria and the economy is showing encouraging signs of growth. Nigeria is also showing its leadership in the region by promoting, in 2001, the creation of a West Africa Free Trade Zone. When fully established this will promote trade between Nigeria and six of its neighbours by removing barriers or charges on the movement of people, goods and services. Nigeria has already shown its leadership in the region in helping to bring about peace in war-torn Liberia and Sierra Leone. Now it must lead the region into the increasingly global economy if it and its neighbours are to prosper. In doing so however, Nigeria must not forget its own problems and in particular the ethnic and religious tensions that remain to be overcome. Creating a unified Nigeria, is, perhaps more than anything else, vital to the future of Africa's greatest nation.

▼ *The enterprise and enthusiasm these young boys show in making their go-carts is perhaps the greatest hope for the future of Nigeria.*

Glossary

Biomass fuels Fuels consisting of biological matter (such as wood, crop stalks, animal dung and collected leaves) or methane gas generated from decomposing biological matter.

Black market The illegal buying and selling of goods, especially if they are rare or valuable.

Bush meat Wild animals such as monkeys and bush pigs which are killed by humans for eating.

Cash crops Crops grown to sell for money. They include crops such as palm oil, groundnuts, cocoa and fruits.

Cholera A disease of the gut, often fatal, caused by swallowing food or water contaminated with bacteria.

Colony A country that is ruled by another country. Nigeria was ruled by Britain until it gained independence in 1960.

Corruption The dishonest use of power, money or goods for personal gain, usually at the expense of the welfare of others.

Desertification A condition whereby soils lose their fertility, for example, as a result of intensive agriculture practices that fail to give soils time to recover between growth cycles, or where topsoil has been lost due to erosion or vegetation removal.

Diarrhoea An illness leading to the passing of watery faeces and dehydration. It is caused by bacterial infection of the gut.

Emir The title given to the ruler of an Islamic region or country.

Exports Products and services sold to foreign countries. For example, oil and palm-oil sold by Nigeria to European countries.

Fossil fuels Fuels from the fossilized remains of plants and animals formed over millions of years. They include coal, oil and natural gas. Once used they are gone – non-renewable.

Gross Domestic Product (GDP) The monetary value of goods and services produced by a country in a single year. Often measured per person (capita) as GDP per capita.

Gross National Product (GNP) The monetary value of the goods and services produced by a country plus any earnings from overseas in a single year. Often measured per person (capita) as GNP per capita.

Harmattan A seasonal, extremely dry, dusty Saharan wind that blows towards the West African coast.

Hijab Clothing worn by Muslim women to cover their head and bodies.

Hydroelectric power (HEP) Electricity generated by water as it passes through turbines. HEP normally involves damming river valleys and forming artificial lakes.

Imports Products and services brought in from an outside country.

Informal economy Goods and services provided by groups and individuals who do not pay taxes to the government.

Inputs Items such as chemical fertilizer and machinery which are used by farmers to improve their crops.

Malaria An infectious tropical disease which is carried by infected mosquitoes. Malaria is common in Africa and parts of Asia.

Micro-credit scheme Sometimes known as 'micro-finance schemes', these are small loans given to individuals or groups to help them start businesses or other income-generating schemes.

Military rule Rule of region or country by a military leader and their forces as opposed to an elected civilian government.

Missionary A person sent by a church to another country to spread their religious faith and beliefs. Missionaries often carry out social and medical work.

Oral Rehydration Therapy (ORT) A treatment used to treat dehydration resulting from diarrhoea. ORT usually involves drinking a solution made from mineral salts dissolved in water.

Organic Relating to living organisms that occur naturally in the environment. Organic substances can be broken down by nature – they are biodegradable.

Pastoralists People who depend primarily on livestock (especially cattle) for their livelihoods. In Nigeria the Hausa-Fulani are the main pastoral group.

Plateau An area of level land found at the summit of a mountain, hill or area of raised land.

Polygamy The custom of having two or more wives at the same time, common in many Islamic cultures.

Protectorate A region or country that is controlled by another more powerful region or country.

Purdah The custom of keeping women separate from the rest of society and covered with clothing, usually from head to foot. Purdah is common in Islamic communities.

Sahel A belt of semi-arid (dry) land that runs across Africa to the south of the Sahara.

Sanitation The provision of hygienic toilet and washing conditions to prevent the spread of diseases associated with human waste.

Secular Not belonging to or associated with any specific religion.

Shanty towns Makeshift settlements close to urban centres. They normally lack basic services and are often built illegally.

Sharia law A religious law, based on the Koran, maintained by Islamic communities.

Soil erosion The removal of soil naturally (by water, wind) or by people (poor agricultural practices, deforestation, overgrazing). This can lead to desertification.

Staple crops Foods that form the basis of people's diets. In Nigeria they include maize and millet.

Terraced farming System where crops are grown on horizontal steps cut into a hillside.

Typhoid A serious, sometimes fatal, disease characterized by a pink rash, which is caused by swallowing food or water contaminated with bacteria.

Further Information

Books

The Ancient World: Benin & Other African Kingdoms
by Sean Sheehan
(Hodder Wayland, 1998)

Economically Developing Countries: Nigeria
by Alasdair Tenquist
(Hodder Children's Books, 1995)

World Fact Files: West Africa
by Tony Binns and Rob Bowden
(Hodder Wayland, 1998)

Useful addresses

Nigeria High Commission
Nigeria House
9 Northumberland Avenue
London
WC2N 5BX
United Kingdom
Tel: 020 7556 8145

Index

Numbers in **bold** are pages where there is a photograph or illustration.